DANIEL IN THE LIONS' DEN

Illustrated by Tony Morris

Brimax · Newmarket · England

Many years ago, the city of Jerusalem was attacked and conquered by King Nebuchadnezzar of Babylon. He returned home with treasure from the Temple of Jerusalem and a group of young men. He wanted to teach these young men about the ways of Babylon.

Among these young men was a boy called Daniel and his three friends Shadrach, Meshach and Abednego. They worked hard and learned all they were taught. King Nebuchadnezzar offered them food and drink from his own table. The four young men preferred the simple diet of their homeland and this pleased God, as it showed how all four remained loyal to him. God then gave Daniel the power to understand peoples' dreams.

One night, King Nebuchadnezzar had a dream which worried him. He called together all his wisemen but no one could explain about the dream. The king was angry and sentenced all his wisemen to death.

When Daniel heard what had happened, he prayed to God for help, then went to see the king.

"I will explain your dream," he said. "You saw a giant statue with a golden head. Its body was made of silver and bronze, its legs and feet of iron and clay. As you looked at the statue, a stone fell on it and smashed it into pieces. Then a stone mountain grew in the statue's place. The statue is your kingdom, which will be conquered and destroyed. The stone mountain is the Kingdom of God, which will grow stronger and stronger and will last forever."

King Nebuchadnezzar could not forget his dream. He decided to make himself a statue of gold and set it up outside the city. When his craftsmen had finished work on the statue, the king ordered all the people of Babylon to gather outside the city and worship the statue.

"When you hear the sound of trumpets," ordered the king, "you must kneel and worship the statue." As the trumpets sounded, everyone fell to their knees, except for three men, Shadrach, Meshach and Abednego.

When the king heard how his order had been disobeyed, he was furious. "If you do not kneel and worship the statue, you will be thrown into a blazing furnace," he cried.

But the three men remained loyal to God and would not kneel.

King Nebuchadnezzar ordered the furnace to be made even hotter than usual. Shadrach, Meshach and Abednego were tied up and thrown into the flames. The heat was so strong that even the guards who threw the men into the furnace were killed by the fire.

The king watched in amazement. "How many men were thrown into the fire?" he asked his servants.

"Three, your majesty," the servants replied.

"I can see four men," said the king. "None are tied up or hurt in any way. The fourth man looks like an angel of God."

The king was right. An angel had been sent by God to protect the three men. When they stepped unhurt from the flames, the king said, "Your God is great."

Some time later, King Nebuchadnezzar had another dream. He saw a great tree which grew bigger and bigger. It could be seen from all over the world and provided everyone with food and shelter. Then an angel came from God and told the king to cut down the tree.

"What does this dream mean?" the king asked Daniel.

Daniel told the king, "Your dream fills me with sadness. You are that tree, providing people with food and protection. But unless you obey God, your power will be taken away and you will become mad."

The king ignored Daniel's words and one day, a terrible madness overcame him. He was thrown out of the city and went to live in the woods and fields. The madness lasted for many years until one day, the king realized that God was more powerful than any king, and was healed.

When King Nebuchadnezzar died, his son Belshazzar became king. He held a great feast and everyone ate and drank from the treasure King Nebuchadnezzar had stolen from the Temple of Jerusalem. As they ate, a hand appeared and wrote a message on the wall. The king was very frightened. He called for Daniel to tell him the meaning of this. Daniel said, "God is not pleased with you. This message means that your kingdom will be conquered by your enemies." That night, King Belshazzar was murdered.

Then Darius became king. He had been an enemy of Belshazzar. He made Daniel ruler over all his governors, because he knew that Daniel was wiser than anyone else in Babylon. The governors were jealous of Daniel and they plotted against him.

A group of governors went to see King Darius. They had a new law for him to sign. This forbade the people to pray to any god for the next thirty days. Anyone found breaking the law would be thrown to the lions. King Darius agreed to sign the law.

Daniel heard about the new law, but he continued to pray to God. One day, his enemies caught him praying. He was taken to the king, who was upset to learn that Daniel had broken the law. He wanted to help Daniel, but knew that he must go to the lions.

King Darius went with Daniel to the lions' pit. He said, "I hope your God can save you."
Then Daniel was thrown into the pit. King Darius returned to the palace and prayed all night for Daniel's safety.

The next morning, the king returned to the pit. "Are you there, Daniel?" he called.
"Yes, I am safe," replied Daniel. "God sent his angel to protect me from the lions' jaws."
The king was very happy that Daniel was safe.

King Darius realized that he had been tricked into signing the law. All the wicked governors who had plotted against Daniel were thrown into the lions' pit. The lions tore them to pieces.

Then King Darius made a new law,
saying that all the people in his
kingdom must worship the God of
Daniel, for he is the the true God.

All these appear in the pages of the story.
Can you find them?

Daniel

Meshach

Shadrach

Abednego